"I love everything about [the collection]. [A]midst the science, the insistent internationality, his iterative considerations of translation, his lingering focus on our ecological crisis, [Jaspreet] Singh manages to write with such an amiable, provocatively thoughtful but direct syntax. The overriding questions the poems ask—Where is the place of the human in geological time? What, if anything, distinguishes "I" from "we-ness"—are the most profound questions of our moment."

—**FORREST GANDER,** Pulitzer Prize-winning author of *Be With*

"Jaspreet Singh is a restless traveller and writer, a chronicler of the magnitude of destruction we exact upon each other and the earth. He's also a lyric chemist, willing to mix genres and play with traditional forms. *Dreams of the Epoch & the Rock* reads like a eureka moment in the lifelong experiment, where the heaviness and inhospitable toxicity of the Anthropocene is lifted, briefly, on the breaks and in the breath."

—**NICK THRAN,** award-winning author of *If It Gets Quiet Later On, I Will Make a Display* and *Earworm*

"Jaspreet Singh's poems correlate despair and loving attention in our age of earth ravage. They do this whimsically, often with humour at human unconsciousness, even as he probes his own unconscious through dream and childhood memory. In lines that extend to prose or shrink to haiku, what shines through is their remarkable accuracy, lucid, immediate to our time. This book speaks to/for so many."

—**DAPHNE MARLATT,** award-winning author of *Ana Historic* and *The Given*

"Extraordinary. These poems spark an inexplicable sensation."

—**KIM NEKARDA,** visual artist, Berlin

"How do you write poetry, as the familiar Earth that nurtured you turns—and turns for real and forever—into a different planet? Jaspreet Singh's evocative, delicately crafted lines explore the rubicon we have all crossed, while never losing sight of human nuance. It's a memorable, thought-provoking collection."

"A book alone cannot repair the world, but, in its shapeshifting dance between hope and loss, fear and affirmation, Jaspreet Singh's *Dreams of the Epoch & the Rock* is a manual for reparation. "Poetry makes some / things happen," asserts "What We Call Beauty," *contra* Auden, in Singh's work by eschewing rhetoric or false lyricism, teaching new words, hovering in far places—the Indus Valley, Andes, Oceania—before extractive capitalism altered them. In these slant poems, ravaged life itself speaks, or dreams aloud, making "Ghost Acoustic Interventions." "If views clash we'll practice / speaking untranslatable words / together," Singh writes in "Iktsuarpok," prodding us to listen as the extra-human world dreams itself. Opening up the spaces between human words, suggesting a million other voices, Singh's is radical version of Keats's Negative Capability, exactly needed at this moment to help us wake from our stale dreams of dominion."

"From coral reefs to Punjabi songs at Tim Hortons, *Dreams of the Epoch & the Rock* transports us to poetic illuminations that are meditative and surprising. Through science, sound, Cervantes, and the geology of Alberta, Singh intersects lyrical ecocriticism with the personal in our moment of climate crises. Singh is a poet of light."

DREAMS

OF THE

EPOCH

& THE

ROCK

BOOKS BY JASPREET SINGH

POETRY

Dreams of the Epoch & the Rock (2024)
How to Hold a Pebble (2022)
November (2017)

MEMOIR

My Mother, My Translator (2021)

NOVELS

Face (2022)
Helium (2013)
Chef (2008)

SHORT STORIES

Seventeen Tomatoes: Tales from Kashmir (2004)

Dreams of the Epoch & the Rock

POEMS

Jaspreet Singh

NEWEST PRESS

Library and Archives Canada Cataloguing in Publication
Title: Dreams of the epoch & the rock : poems / by Jaspreet Singh.
Other titles: Dreams of the epoch and the rock
Names: Singh, Jaspreet, 1969– author.
Series: Crow said poetry.
Description: Series statement: Crow said poetry
Identifiers: Canadiana (print) 20230586023 | Canadiana (ebook) 20230586031 | ISBN 9781774391082 (softcover) | ISBN 9781774391099 (EPUB)
Subjects: LCGFT: Poetry.
Classification: LCC PS8637.I53 D74 2024 | DDC C811/.6—dc23

Editor for the Press: Laurie Graham
Book design: Natalie Olsen, Kisscut Design

NeWest Press wishes to acknowledge that the land on which we operate is Treaty 6 territory and a traditional meeting ground and home for many Indigenous Peoples, including Cree, Saulteaux, Niitsitapi (Blackfoot), Métis, Dene, and Nakota Sioux since time immemorial.

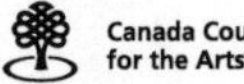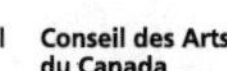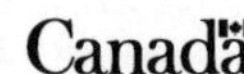

NeWest Press acknowledges the support of the Canada Council for the Arts, the Alberta Foundation for the Arts, and the Edmonton Arts Council for support of our publishing program. This project is funded in part by the Government of Canada.

#201, 8540 – 109 Street
Edmonton, Alberta T6G 1E6
780.432.9427
NeWest Press www.newestpress.com

No bison were harmed in the making of this book.
Printed and bound in Canada

We sit together, the mountain and me,
until only the mountain remains.

— **Li Bai,** 701–762

CONTENTS

DREAMS

OF THE

EPOCH

& THE

The palm leaf a child made
With chalk on asphalt is still
In my mind Now and then it is

Erased by rain
Because that is what rain is
And now and then the palm

Leaf
Returns as a palm forest
Because that is what a child is

— Evening recitation —

My father is expected
any minute. I am
waiting at the airport
in Edmonton
by the Tim Hortons. The woman
who served me
Timbits was speaking
in Punjabi to her colleague. And
now the table
next to me breaks
into a song
in Punjabi. Sometimes
I find it hard
to distinguish between a sacred
and a secular
song. Perhaps it is neither
or both—

Ude ud aave se kosa
tis paacche bachre chharya
tin kavan khalave kavan chugaave…
There are birds, they fly from far-
away lands to escape bitter winters,
they leave the children behind, who feeds their young?
The announcement says
my father's flight is ten minutes
late. Most likely due to the wind's
direction

I sit at the feet
of that direction
like that boy five

       years old   their train car pulled by coal's
                   steam
comes to an unexpected
stop   F is for Father, his
father steps out   When wheels
roll again he's still   not back

'All my, all my fault'
The boy's inner life begins
                  with guilt
He keeps looking at the faces and shadows
around him
until the prayer's   answered

He will forget
he had wondered
about the efficaciousness
of that palm-folded prayer
So happy   it is going to rain
Inside the train he has two
           fathers
one who just offered him a Turkish sweet and the other
who's watching him eat

CORAL SCIENTISTS

> *You grieve*
> *Not that heaven does not exist but*
> *That it exists without us*
>
> —W.S. Merwin

Scientists revived   a coral reef
by playing recordings of sounds   the reef made
when it was teeming with life   *A sound idea*   When young
fish   faraway   heard
the proof they swam   to the site   and star-
ted returning the dead and near dead back to life

Gai[a]—the technique was affectionately named
Ghost Acoustic Interventions One intervention-
ist said if we Sapiens don't change our ways
we might end up summoning the ghosts over
and over   But one day the sea creatures will learn
Learn to hear better and will not return

WITHOUT BEDS, LIFE WOULD BE A MISTAKE

A firm bed   our bed
half canyon half koan
Night comes to us but
it's the bed
that makes us
acknowledge G
& kinship
with g Sharpens
our T-cells for future's
lessness Often
puts our ears to deep
past The epoch
and the rock They wake
us to repair flaws
in air's circulation
We bind our I-nesses Co-
laborate with breath Float up
as in a Tarkovsky We sleep
become embryos again
to learn that we belong
to a pack that can
never assume the planet
as a given We stare
we stare at eyes
of those we call
animals Our bed
all beds try level
best but every crack
of dawn we tear our-
selves apart eager
to forget the strange
things we got so near

Last night you said when you hear me breathe you hear yourself breathe and you feel seized by a thought recurring. Why have we created an excess of emotion when it comes to dinosaurs when we have almost no emotion for the Great Oxygenation Event some 2.4 billion years ago? Is it because bacteria were the heroes? We know all breath comes out of that. Yet, we, who design our lives around ownership and agency, disavow. Build no rooms for certain affects because we fear the bacteria will leave us with no option but to acknowledge. Sapiens come so late in the history of things. Neither the planet nor the bacteria created oxygen keeping us or our opera halls in mind. All along Earth was not slowly "getting ready to receive us." Last night your breath had acquired the same rhythm as mine. Everything was so synchronized. It calmed us almost calmed us down.

Great poet Faiz Ahmad Faiz visited Saskatoon light years ago. I stumble into two who remember. They don't share the things I'm really after. One shows me an empty bottle of rum, another dissects the pizza they ate after the mushaira. Both have forgotten the poems he recited. Both emit a strange light. I try to catch the light and fall down and don't break a single bone. I try to catch the light and fall down and don't break a single bone.

The tea almost gone
from our cups   Ulla
took off her glasses
Said she met Tomas Tranströmer
in his house in Sweden
Schubert was playing
The moment he appeared
she'd bowed almost genuflected
as if a saint walked in The smile
on his lightly embarrassed
face betrayed nothing about
the recently lost hat   and
the stroke he had suffered
which left parts of the body
paralyzed Schubert kept playing
cooling the room
until the host turned
the radio off
got himself wheeled to the well-
lit corner and played for her
the piano with his left hand

MY GODS

> *Silence is the invention of the hearing.*
>
> —Ilya Kaminsky

There is silence
  known only by sounds

Sounds
  that only silence knows

The place where they witness
  each other—the shrine of my gods

Soon more pilgrims will come
  half-expecting the doors open

My gods say to me You are but a few shovels
  of atoms wandering together

Wander well
  Wander with thoughtful delight

And for a millionth time
  I depart For a millionth time they

repeat: What the thunder said
  is nothing

compared to what it didn't   say

A HOLOCENE POEM

— After William Carlos Williams —

You were fast asleep when I raised the heat
by 3.5 degrees because I'd a sudden
craving to eat the juicy mangoes my
cousin sent us all the way from Punjab

I thought they'd taste more succulent if the room
were warmer and they did I am sorry
if the thermostat adjustment caused any dis-
comfort So tender
& sweet those thirteen mangoes

I love those incomprehensible flamingoes
beating wings then bowing

and feel something similar to wonder
facing an insect preserved in yellow amber

I've accepted failure
to locate correct form
to understand grass and flowers

that bide for decades in drylands
as dormant seeds

What language do they speak?
What do they call
what I call waiting for rain?

WINDOW

The lake is a window
to the Earth—wrote
the Baltic poet

when most
poets had forgotten
the Earth

His words
gestate inside
me as I

drive to Crawford
Ontario
to dunk a finger

in the lake
where the Anthropocene might've left
unfaint

marks of its beginning No window
opened
but ever since

ghosts

have been
emitting signals

in a language I am

only now beginning
to speak   half
speak

                        —*July, 2023*

EARTH SCIENCES

I.

In Kamakura where the Buddha is almost the size of a mountain
the Anthropocene Working Group has gathered in a four-
storey hotel In the day the geologists debate
the mark of the new epoch   In the night they listen to Schubert
Each one in their own room with card keys and a little sand on feet
oblivious to Buddha's eye   ear   tongue
How old is the world? a monk had asked the enlightened one once
How long an eon? Kalpa?

II.

One geologist sits alone in her air-conditioned room *String*
Quintet   Adagio   A blue bandanna
entangles her hair Outside the window ocean waves
form and break Like others she an exemplar
in her subfield Inventor of a new-gen stethoscope
to listen to Earth's depths and shallows Even in landlocked hamlets
she can listen to the far away ocean tides surge and recede

III.

On page three a local paper addresses 'the state
of the haiku' as if 'the state of the weather' Up
until now the poetic form relied on each season's stable arrival
and departure Some confusion has set in among the young practitioners How
does one in the new era achieve the perfection of Bashō or Issa?

I seem to have lived Two dozen summers This long winter

IV.

On FaceTime the geologist now talks to her daughter
On a different continent the five-year old would like to speak
some day to a whale She shows her ma crayon drawings
of whales   *And what language would you speak in?*
Don't you even know this, silly? Whales don't
live in our language, Ma   Even my younger sister knows we will
need translators She's right, thinks the geologist Sperm whales "click"
low-frequency waves Within the species messages go back
and forth by way of some enigmatic Morse code

V.

During the banquet dinner the Anthropocene Working Group
generates an uncanny hum While eating greens
the geologist learns all she missed The keynote
about a Canadian site with *a golden spike* But then she's alone
again in the crowd thinking about water
hoping her daughters take her along   wanting to
witness the exchange   *What will the whales say?*
Perhaps the whales could help us find a sound
way out of this mess Perhaps they're already
saying things Things we don't want
to put our ears on or see Back in her room overwhelmed she
fell asleep   You are
                    where your dream is

The day we will solve the wicked problem was already behind us
    Imagined deimagined reimagined unimagined
overimagined by untold numbers   it accompanied
    each one of us   no matter what startle
the quotidian brought No matter where we were
    land water air technosphere stratosphere   and our
level of complicity What geoglyphs we shaped Or silenced
    Always a step ahead   the day
dissolved imminent peril We couldn't touch blue
    but "blue" oceans repaired   "green"
forests   the original "brown" glint   Some said
    the day was nothing less than lithic
light   Our doubts   it put them in a vase
    like hydrangeas
until they wilted   A new

language was born
No empires its models   no equestrian
    statues for old colonial masters
From a distance we admired the day's
    faithful translations on
bilingual sea pages   and those
    perfervid skies (owned by none) got close
closer   and time
thickened   The day consoled
    our desolations   re-centred meaning   put on left
shoulders an ally's invisible hand
    Removing its toque it promised
us its ear
    Yet we forgot we owed every-
thing to it beginning
    with breath   Struggled
to remember what lay outside
    memory   We stepped on

stones with past's pink
    veins   and boudins   discarded heat
in permafrost Picked
    ourselves up Nothing escaped now
we upped speed   fell in and out
    of old style love again   bought
& sold water   made self-
    learning algorithms
out of coal   all was
    possible   again
great acceleration   greed rose
    up to our necks & neocortices
the illusion that we controlled
    even the shadows It was
then the day began
    unbuilding
breaking falling behind Covered its eyes
    with what felt like nubbed ribbons
of loss An endling's
    last triumph
gone—

the day showed us its tongue   lignifying
Some of us offered spare
    rooms   but it wanted to go   down
in history as an unremembered
    thing   like specks
of phosphorous   on the tip
    of an abandoned matchstick, almost night
Those born in light's absence
    grasped the kinks
of complexity They couldn't not
In granite dark they lit a small
    flame and the wisest
we can do right now is to walk
    with them

MEDITATION

Little birds walking on fresh snow

Five of nine sapiens
already live in the post-
apocalyptic   So who's

        "we"

in poems
and in the world?

The person thinking such
thoughts is not unimplicated
No one is

Little birds walking on fresh snow
staring at me
 staring at them

It said to me all metaphor
    (including this)
a delusion   a frozen
  lake

is neither honey-
  comb nor eye glass
Evenings aren't blue-
  black berries

The real is animated flesh
  nerves, toenails, blood
Metaphor is mere
  Madame Tussauds

In no way this imp-
  lies
one ought to give
  up making

poems   a labour
  as indispensable as maths
and silence   It held
  my hand before parting   Spoke
a different geontology
  In stones
and between them wander things

we will neither be able to name
nor word

My breath condensed
  on old photographs
of my mother
  Her mother   her mother's
mother

As always it watered the tulsi
  plant on the balcony I heard
retreating footsteps   steps taken
  by feet   *Your*
relationship with water
  seems less than
ideal You must
  reform your withness with
it Water is
  not like some slippery supple
worm   *or a wound*
  repairer   *Memory's*
oblivioner   *or keeper*
  Water is

Language is a window. Strawberries taste different when one stands by different windows. Language is a hallucination. Barbershops trigger different affects in Spanish, Punjabi, Cree. Grass grows at a different speed. Sometimes I smell earth in the lemon trees of a new language. Hear the world. For the first time. The new language's poets make me realize there are horses with six legs. In streets or trains or mercados the rising sun of its advanced speakers makes my ears go heliotropic. Now I have more ways to describe light when it contacts leaves that it helped make. More memory pathways to childhood's blood oranges. More vocabularies of love and its impossibility. Coal, carbón. Lluvia, rain. Sangre, blood. Sometimes I wish the new language (like the old) didn't come stained by histories. Erasing entire peoples. But soon. I learn the new language's own wounds and pronounce the diminutive of "now"—ahorita. Sit alone. I will never know if I have more empathy in language X or language Y. But I might develop more. Because both X and Y talk to each other. Within me. Beautiful word. Parpadeo. I sleep in the nest of the language I am learning. Eventually it will learn more about me than I will about it. Eventually time will heal wounds. Eventually wounds will heal time. Eventually strawberries will disappear from my dream. I will wake up thirsty. Stand by the window. The sea is not far. El mar no está lejos.

Strange day it was between two nights
Borges had hired me to read him
a second hand liquid-marked Cervantes
Old telegraph wires tangoed

now and then in the wind I was worried I was
misreading
& misunderstanding
the perturbed pages. Borges said
Sigue enriqueciendo el texto
Keep enriching the text

Borges is not a good person
He keeps persuading ravens
to change his epitaph
His words erode and brecciate
rock. He refused to buy me
seafood paella. Says there's no such
thing as seafood paella

THE WORD

"I" is not so lonely
In my mother
Tongue

And "Mother"
And "I"
Begin with the same

Consonant
Here, I'm not
Thinking

About language *x* or *y*
As our only home
I'm saying this is

How a moment
Of lucidity
Holds my hand

When I unthink
In my non-mother
Tongue

THE FOREST

— After Yusef Komunyakaa —

The forest is burning like an ancient book
Burning like Toba and Tambora
Burning like a million incense sticks in a temple
Burning like a familiar hospital
Burning like Surya's seventh horse
Burning like an enigma: *Should trees have standing?*
Burning like a word uttered by Agni
Burning like a yellow-robed monk self-immolating
Burning like stones in Hiroshima
Ash is an oracular colour
Ash is an oracular colour

HIGH LEVEL BRIDGE

The first night you looked like a canvas
Vermeer never painted. Because the Rhine had gone
to sleep. The second night like those noisy
precarious railway tracks
over the Ganga. When my gaze fell
on you midday you were up to your neck
        engaged in arguments
        with the inebriated 20th-century
until a passing newspaper threw its ink on blunt crystals
of ice. The century's heavy-lidded eyes summarized you
as a dream or a coffin. You disagreed
with the contact lens old woman in a red jacket as well
who was quietly studying your weathered cast iron
dots and dashes as if in them was written the river's future
        and the city's too
Only then I saw the higher thing
you witness every other day. The old woman's hand
        on the shoulder
of the young woman who didn't jump

CHAIRS

Many a time I forget them
until a friend leaves
my place after a longish catching-
up dinner

I look at her chair
the way she left it behind
Facing a rare direction
the chair freshly empty
Still carrying
heavy things
she didn't want to tell

or couldn't

After I am done I sit
in her chair
until the new dawn
staring at my chair

aspiring
to make contact

with the mild creaking
of ungraspable things

the ones I find
difficult really
difficult to share with her
with myself

We are rereading the same book
in Spanish. The passages ignored last time
made us pause

"… as if time were not a river
but an earthquake happening nearby"

Nothing else shook us the rest of
the summer. It must be real
hard work for time
to always go through
in a liquid state   when it could be a mountain
rising or eroding
Or a thread
going through a needle

    September arrived. Strong
winds are blowing outside   I stare
a lot at the piece of basalt
on my desk
and try to reread
Time's Arrow, Time's Cycle

But for no reason

my mind drifts toward women
and men   in ancient India
who blessed newborn babies by passing
them through perforated stones

Mostly when I write poems I don't ask who might
read them. Today unable to make that leap
I feel like a waiter in an almost empty restaurant
taking a tray of coffee and cookies to a table
that never ordered

Once in my youth I served
a shy prof who kept folding-unfolding
the napkins
to reveal the geologic. Faults   he called

them. The table adjacent to his   more vibrant
Half holding   the dangling cloth
the family's little child
had just figured how to walk

Papa needed a shave and Mama needed sleep
New mountains rose on their proud faces
and the child kept going further and further away
Kept going

I

Dreamt I was a bowdlerized rock
Dreaming I was a tiny

Camera on the ankle of a gyrfalcon

— Edward Burtynsky, *Basque Coast #3*, UNESCO Geopark, Zumaia, Spain (2015) —

When will the sunbathing tourist couple
look at the bare rock
behind them?

So imposing the behind-scape, one's ears
encounter the rustle of clichés
'sublime' 'enchantment' ' uncanniness'

The woman, shivers
circle her spine
as she eyes a ghost written memoir

The man, his monologues surf
silently in a different zone, he sniffs
crystals of lighter air

The rock belongs
to a different scale. It
was birthed in the deep   ocean   Two languages
it speaks Language
of time and language
of witness. It has been
through high coolings & warmings Preserves
within   the grey-
bearded archive of past's extremes

The couple will not turn
until five suns rise
and one million Icaruses fall
down from the sky
Every day they'll sit
at the exact same exact same
Salt-air will print Yohoia
on their diminishing necks   every dusk
        the sea
will amplify its own pensiveness   break
                                    then still

I find this photograph terrifying
                        I am that couple

And is that my father's opened beard
I am seeing?
I put on my thick
glasses and it's mere chimney smoke
going up and down like dots & unbroken lines
    in
graphs of geologic time now saying yes and
Yes to extinction, now saying no and No

I like people like you the silent types, said the cab
driver   Are you coming back from a holiday?

Centuries ago a boat from X made it to Z. Refuge was a certain
ambiguity. *Look at this tall glass of milk. Full to the brim.*
To which the whole boat said—Add us like sugar to the glass

The shadow of a metallic bird fell on me and I couldn't help but think about the
woman who hopes to leave her homeland but cannot and the man who does
not desire but must And they who have no homeland

I identified with their faces I identify Sometimes I seriously identify with the
ones obliged to return after separation's long years to the grand myth of 'my
country'

They grip me those who candidly see through the candy made by 'enlightened
places'

They try to persuade—'life is nothing but this' or 'life is nothing but that'—the
ones who wear history's crumpled clothes and revisit past losses with children
born elsewhere

If I add some heard sadnesses—and human kindnesses given and received—to
vats of colour and out of that spin a thread I'd be able to weave an intricate
carpet

and sitting on it   understand the one who moved   the one who stayed

But her place

kept changing Some said it

was no longer   a place

Shall I change the form then? Someone insists all I can do is change
forms

I'm walking in half gale half storm   Last winter's sidewalk
grit flies around me   What epoch does it belong to
                    the particle that just entered my eye?

I'll keep gathering
                    evidence   boats
sinking   ice calving   rings
of boreal fire   as if it were a child's
Pixar

                                        They whisper

in my ears   my wistful guests the ghosts

The forest of affluent smoke & ash
in your city   is
                    real

Smell it they say   This the smell of deep time

PAWN SHOP

There is a fancy pawn shop in my city
You can sell your dreams
there. The hidden reason one visits
that phantasmagoric collection
is the chocolate
cat called Harley. On the same day
you can acquire a palm-size meteorite
and a cactus
rainstick. You can sell an old dial radio
a cello
with or without a red velvet case
Over the years the stoic owner's face
has come to resemble Harley's
In a rare glass case he has on display
cigar boxes
preowned by long dead oil
executives, a 1912 Mandarin
primer, a tender gambling
spinner... Although mostly out
of stock, once in a while you can
buy ruby slippers
coated with gleams of cat hair
They'll lift your mood. You'll find
yourself deciphering the words
hurling out of that paw-
polishing tongue, and right
then Harley will meet
your gaze and ask: What's economy?
What's air?   And you can finally emerge
back into the city   carrying that

Close your eyes Imagine an apple
The scientist scanned
a burst of electric
activity in my brain

The apple I saw
was the one
that began my childhood at Nishat
in Kashmir Grandma
in a pherozi stream
was already washing it
Her unironed face
smiling on behalf of the earth
I described the bite the crunch
the taste the honey smell

The scan had ended
not the apple Warm like
air held in my winter's layers

On a familiar branch
it was ripening Some friends
were taking turns, smelling
my apple Old
leaves

kept falling
on us like schools
of fish Little by little
our bodies

changed and were gone
But the apple
remained just the same

ripening

When I moved to the new city I hoped people would be real
different Flags
high on copper roofs Salt waiting for snow
on sidewalks   Some buildings textures of red
sandstone   others pure
glass   I walked the streets
in cheap footwear and despairing
socks   By the bus-stop two
men reeked of stout   the older
one unfond of slow hockey
and slow cars In the used
bookstore a woman was lost
in a 19th century Russian novel
At the art-deco cinema a shady
character puffed a Winston
"It's forbidden" I mustered courage
"I know" he intoned and continued
 sending wispy toxins
In a metro car silence sat between
a musician's attenuated band-aid
fingers and the strings
of his lute   She left me speechless
the nonagenarian recycling
lemons & Audubons
Near the zoo I slipped badly
a fur coat clad passerby
gave me his hand
By the half frozen river a child was crying
Most likely a misplaced toy
But the loss monumental

Sometimes it feels only
two minutes have passed by
      I weigh the haze
of numerous gone   years
and with deepened embarrassment
confess   the people in the new
city turned out more or less
like the ones left behind

and all I can do is come
to a gentle acceptance

I.

These days a tooth-ache lasts
  la eternidad

and lifting a latte
  cup means lifting a gym

Now and then both my hands
  go

out on an occasional spin
  My generous colleague

she makes it sound better
—limbs breaking into involuntary dance

But, is it
  dance?

II.

Nothing's natural
not even water   in one's eye
and that time when oceans
  & icefields had no names
swings like a foot
bridge between me and the dead
I hear mastodons
while trance wandering
in West Edmonton Mall

III.

Who is this "I"?

When I crave chocolate, it is not-I,
but the craving

of microbes in my gut

Is it "us"?

Is it "we-ness"?

IV.

"Where will you go today?" I ask
my ninety-five-year-old

neighbour
"Wherever
the ecstatic stick
will take me"

V.

The face of the other
And the genes
        of the other

Biologists say Sapien
DNA
 —mostly the DNA of Other   species

So it is

hard science not mysticism
 —Others live in me and I live
in them

Not absence of body but its celebration
My soul is a milky way of images swallowed
and gulped   It moos
sometimes malfunctions
Parallel lines of border guards and refugees
knock on its soft door
At times a sudden yeti
stands on it barefoot
Every afternoon it is a warm bee
buzzing
ancestors—helpful guides
and pure obstacles

So much about it still
an enigma The way it cleanses itself with long dead
languages   In its tiniest room
   prayer

I doubt my soul
has hair or calcium   But it must be
a mammal It sweats the nights I think
I pretty much deciphered the world

Mostly it is sad
but when my soul is happy
it is happy as a well-
aged father   running
toward the rust gate
to hug the child who after thirty
years has returned home

How could I? Upon arrival in Canada I ended up as empire's lumber

An ancestor of mine wrote these words in a slim diary
I am standing by the same lake he stood by almost a hundred years ago
It might freeze any minute now but I won't
walk on it I am lumbering
something similar   thinking about mountains
of discarded ski-boots & high-fashion
clothes in the Atacama desert
Almost a hundred years ago my ancestor had walked out
of the mill almost walked out a troubled man he was almost
valiant We rarely talk
or laugh together When we do
it's always the desert It grows and grows
his voice in the wind and I plug my ears with sand

KUNSTHAUS

Not his self-portraits, not the artist's reclining figures, peculiar
obsession with sex, ears reduced to shape and size of dried fruit
What really stood out was a little tree
Egon Schiele had painted merely six years before the Spanish
influenza. Light was not falling
on the tree the tree was not
reflecting it either. The austere little thing was its own sun radiating
I stood there and there
longer than the guard expected. Hours later
on the train to Vienna the tree
accompanied me as a choric voice. In the hotel room
leaves sprouted from my arms   fingers   ears
I knew this was going to happen. I let it happen

I read an ancient poet   the season turns
he writes
same confusion erupts again

he stands almost naked
eyes closed
under the ambiguous sun
spring or autumn?

birds not confused
oaks not confused
not confused the bumblebees

only we are, he writes
we don't
even know how to stand

like a tree
grow like roots fly
like a bumblebee

Right now both asleep
The tree and the man
with an axe

...

Real joy — I look
for dry socks
and find them dry

...

I stand in front
of the master's paintings   I hear
water's inner life

...

Only Basho's frog
can make me fall
into silence

The plankton
altered the story I am
            and will be

...

Reflecting about
the quality of light
a bougainvillea

...

Come here crane Stretch
your neck Stretch
my potential to change

...

Dragonfly—
are you thinking too
about the Earth?

PAUSE ME

Midnight. The Aurora Borealis
astonished No idea if I was
              awake

or asleep
Dry rain of electric
un-hierophanic green

Pause me, rain
Tonight I
don't want to think any-

thing other
than the trace of "good"
that remains within

me and my
species
In a cabin I

toss, unturn
Somewhere in my oldening
memories my grandmother is shelling
peas

Peace arrives fleetingly by way
of such images   I'm
unable to hold too much

certainty & coherence

To praise the world
or to be a witness?

Two different
languages,
grammars

But with each passing Aurora
I feel both
come from a common

ancestor   And already
my skin is erupting
with a beautiful disease

SEAGULLWARDS

I.

Sister, I love the window And the drops On the window

That Buddha statue Everyone wonders Half-finished, or a ruin?

He's mining the deep sea She's looking Seagullwards

White Anthropocene Black Anthropocene Brown Anthropocene …

Under eighty billion objects Eight billion Skulls

Still alive Lichen And the cat

Wet day My thoughts Are noodles

II.

Neem tree In its shade one is Caressed by grandma

Fog on glasses Hard to see That nothing in the doughnut

Fog in ears Hard to hear That nothing between waves of water

Slowness in Stratosphere Will take hours To land on radishes

In the orchard A murmur and a rumour Collect trace evidence

Singh was the man Who ate apples In the Anthropocene

I.

Great wind will blow from Yukon or Yucatan
the day we depart
                              It will scatter

seeds on the freshly dead   Clouds
will hammock
street walking forests   Species

hope & memory will rock
inside teapot minerals   Coal
houses will run and roll back

like pebbles in a river
In left-behind
toolboxes every nail   a carnival

of rust and flow   Sometimes
lyrebirds will tell stories
in their songs

II.

The desert's not a wasteland
Now I know
how to put the stethoscope
in my ear, listen
to arid ecosystems
The Taj Mahal is falling down
The Taj Mahal is falling down
and the desert's   not
a wasteland

III.

Now I learn from the lichen
by my verandah
following earth's time
Now from the little girl
who chalks
palm leaves on asphalt
Now from phytoplankton
in the ocean Staying alive is possible
—it stammers to tell
from eonic experience—
only by keeping others
                    alive
Radically alive

You don't have such words in your language
You don't have such words in your language

After years of wandering
I find myself in a cabin

With a door that for no reason
Keeps anticipating another arrival

Caetano's song is playing again
But I am busy

Figuring out
Some efficient way to cry

If I had children
I would be talking

Exactly like my friend
Those days when we used to drink wine

She told me about the Aymara people
To say 'Don't look back'

To them one must translate it
As 'Don't look ahead'

They face the past
The future is behind them

And behind them
I'm standing on sand in my father's skates

LOPON-LA

— to my sister —

Lopon-la a Tibetan monk saw the Dalai Lama
after spending 18 years
in a Chinese prison

Lopon-la, were you afraid of anything?
Yes there was one thing I was
afraid I might lose
compassion for the Chinese

I was afraid
I spent the last nine hours with Lopon-la
I even imagined a Chinese person
saying the same during
the times of opium
Afraid that she or he might lose compassion
for the British

All night my thought kept
turning to Lopon-la
but also to sapiens
and kinship between species   all
night I struggled
to extend that

admirable path of Lopon-la
But there were moments
I was really afraid

I felt I was on a strange
tarmac

running after planes

taking off one by one

I.

There is a path
  I thought
All along oblivious
  I was making one
On the summit the villagers
  told me

II.

The solar panels smile like an ancient god
Sitting in the lotus posture

It was 12:30 am during our last encounter

I remember
Only two things The teeth had a sheen

and God was eating large bites of darkness

III.

The storm began

so as to catch a dozen
insects bugging the man

sitting alone in a room
(azulejo room)

saying to himself
(and to the scarecrow)

I am not responsible

After reading the book I borrowed I try to sleep. The book described a faraway island. In that culture when a strong emotion strikes people try to sleep.

v.

Dream within a dream   in a sealed red-and-black bag
I deliver menu food ordered by posh Berliners
from a restaurant
in Tuvalu. Tuvalu

submerged but I delivered and got a tip

VI.

Light said
If they no longer
Come to me I shall go
To the moths

VII.

Eating apples in the Anthropocene means eating fossil fuels

Wait something sounds wrong this one is not a dream

VIII.

Stranger, if you translate
These lines into some other tongue
Snow will fall in Arizona

IX

Every night

the same

three poets knock on my door
Lorca, Du Fu, Farrokhzad
Last night I'd not even finished my glass
of milk They gave me a silk cloth

to rub a craggy kalpa   The kalpa
doesn't speak back
in lines
in lines
in lines

X.

Quetzalcoatlite sky

Sea urchins and acids wake up next to me

I err   Where's my hand
that vanished millions of years ago

Between the living and the dead   a dust
window

of time   My mother
says   Poets have never been innocent

Don't you ever forget this

XI.

I had just started unpacking childhood's mirrors
 —broken replicas of Mohenjo-daro's Priest-King and Dancing Girl—
when the era changed
Mehr Licht!
Mehr Licht!
More light
More light
Now there's an excess of light
We three see nothing

XII.

Mother, the three verses you wanted
        me to   I did learn by heart
        as if you lived inside them
        Pavan guru Pani pita Mata dharat mahat

        After the accident
        forgetting began
        In the hospital room   clot by clot
        I forgot them all

        Out of me   the verses
        now reside in the berry fields
        I see them through
        the window They have
        given the fruit a bluish glow

The pyro-cumulus
      clouds in my city walk
in through
      the exits. The moon
tonight will be the slim beak
      of a curlew

XIV.

I sink in Gasoline Alley

The cellar door opens shuts opens shuts

I sketch an atoll   I am an atoll

The geologist Glikson
hammers my coralrocks

I eavesdrop his stream
of consciousness

*Having lost a sense of reverence toward Earth, there is no evidence humans
are about to rise above the realm of perceptions, dreams, myths, legends
and denial...*

I try to hold onto water
What water? Didn't we tell you?

XV.

Phagocenenaufragoceneanglocenephronoceneagnotocenethermocenecapitalocenethalassoceneanthrobscenechthuluceneplantationcenesymbiocenetechnocenethanatocene…

XVI.

The pathologist tore my body open and found

the petal

a friend   lost ages ago

Petal, will I live a long life?
You will live a life

Petal, will the sea survive?
The deep sea will survive

Petal, will a whale talk to me?
It is

Petal, what is that sound?
I am still inside your sleep

I.

Only the eyes
of children saw

little birds
kept returning to

where the tree was

II.

My morning
window Light descends

like cello strings
coming out of a dark case

Two ravens where the tree
was

Hard to decipher
their discourse

One moves
close to the other

Shares a thought
in Beakese

Flies

away   No idea how
the abandoned one feels   will

feel

III.

All day it rained
I reread the art historian
an admirer of water

painted by Rembrandt in 1654
A Woman Bathing in a Stream
Doing water in oil

the hardest test
for painters then
Those tiny white strokes

painted on translucent
skin of water the bather
just stepped into   make us

experience the ripples
intimately   the way her legs
might have experienced

as if we happened upon
a moment eyes should
not see

IV.

Neither nudity nor nakedness
this doesn't belong

to the curator's categories

A woman
stands waist deep in salt

water to catch
a tiny fish. This in Bengal

her only way to earn
a living. Eleven
hours seven
days a week So much

standing in the estuary   fungus
infected
her reproductive organs

She prays

The gods listen
no longer   Doctors charge
an arm and a leg

Their docktory
a fake   She knows

She's the fish
her hands keep
trying to catch

v.

For eight years
For eight years
the news you streamed
made you
believe the fish the woman
didn't exist

Now you know
now what?

VI.

Half of us eight billion
asleep, the other half
resemble hieroglyphs
of dog days
in a glyph dream
Lutes in concert halls
                Lush
pollutants elsewhere
Threads
of violence tangle codas
of enchantment   Deep past
leaves us giddy
and already we
imagine the future   haunted
by the phantasmal
us   Clarity
comes late
or not   Sometimes
rising to meet us
  as a question
  different
from the one about planetary debts
Where have the bees
Gone

VII.

She was real the geologic woman

Two artists drove narrow
   for hours hoping to inter-
view What was it
like to live in Rosebud, Alberta?
   One night thirsty the woman had turned
   on the kitchen tap

Fire flowed out instead

The methane in her water had a thing
or two to do
   with fracking   happening nearby.
   Rosebud
ain't the original bud. Holding her head
in hands she spoke—

Of deletion Hydraulic fracturing erases *water*

   Earth
     quakes in Rosebud
   I don't know the physics—one artist
   to the other—but understand
deletion   They had to
take the detour, go through
   a tunnel, a different country-
   highway back, and this

Time they noticed

    the metamorphic sign
    planted by the big company
'ThankYou for visiting Rosebud'
    Methane
    rolled down their lips
    and flowed into art

VIII.

In old films they wore
fat tuxedoes

their mouths always
sucking

big smoke-
eaten cigars

Now the filthy
rich men
shown as astronauts

in NASA-suits   flying to Mars

IX.

In the new climate
How does one

Live the questions now?

x.

It is like offering half of everything
to gods
        but not quite
A distinguished biologist boiled it
        down to basics:
sapiens must devote half
the earth
to nature, leave
exactly half
to large animals, plants, in-
        vertebrates, above all
to the nourishers of all
        ecosystems:
        bacteria & half under-
stood microbes

XI.

What will he tell the woman
in the estuary
in Bengal?

XII.

Not to end it
with burnt toast
  or with growing concern
for my daughter son
  nephew niece

A storm is brewing
  inside all of us big
as the one outside
  Nothing settled
yet

XIII.

Other than a scrawl
  on wallpaper
—Deep time is time
that can not be erased

In all likelihood the note was hurriedly made
    yet as a command it glowed   as an expectation
earnest above all its persuasive form
    was tied with a string to the corner
of an empty bench in the safe outskirts
    In the absence of wind I might have walked
on Most work still unfinished My shoes worn
    equal parts with worry and distance
Yet I couldn't help but liberate that marvellous
    thing fluttering not counting its days
There was nothing to read between the
    lines only one   and those five painterly words
like a natural gathering of leaves
    in September light Why not perhaps I
    the intended recipient? Ever since I have
walked all the streets and bridges in the town
    Occupied every other wayward bench
Even ate at a table for two at the Macondo
    Where are you?

From up there a pine cone
fell a little ahead
of me as I was
brisk walking   on asphalt
it bounced up
high as me

But it was that little child
who took it home!

If the world were ideal I would write
a poem in which I do not take a line
for a walk

I would make the line elope
all schools of form

and stand on the edge
of a canyon It will

stare deep and deep and deep and deep and ask
what is this greatest show on earth all about

At midnight the poem would beam
the line onto nearby cliffs and I will lose

fear of some day making it
to the only rock I can hold   onto

Yes it is
then I will head back *to a present where I have never been*

and time will alter   my sense of time
will alter

THE RED-CROWNED CRANE

has come back from near
extinction
in the DMZ

My friend
our long separation
will soon be

over   Is that why
I see those
white-naped cranes   nearby

If the two
Koreas
were to   reunify

they say the development
would kill
the cranes

They pierce me
the low-

pitched purrs bugles   moans   hisses   cackles   persistent
calls

those loud kar-r-r-o-o-o-s
My ears run
a little ahead

as I walk to the dive
bar where you said
you might be

I turn
back?
I don't turn back?

ICE BODIES

— Ice bodies found in Manitoba —

Now that we are ice even nights chime more like a Cambrian explosion Stars bow as they enter frosty cracks of our eyelids When alive just months ago we wore strange names Lacked even tarpaulin And that crevasse called a country Wolves howled Wolves howl Four bodies we are on the frigid Canadian Shield Two adult migrants Two children Ours

Remembered things are not the only truth But even truth is not enough to set one free The white here the waywardness of a building storm Creamy skin of rimed milk at minus fifty-nine about to boil Wind blows like voices of bazaar vendors but we don't know what they're saying Spit congeals in mouths sewn by needles of ice Minerals turn out noisier than we expect Crystals stab little warmth History erodes itself in a parenthesis Where is that music coming from? It is the kind one hears only when one learns to unhear the heard The stratigraphic rarely hides its sacred tapus Beneath us: absences, absences above all absences of the sedimentary Stone is not the right word The *rock* here smells of Hades' fires   Implacable igneous-&-metamorphic ensures earthquakelessness The Canadian Shield speaks of a nation more substantial than this nation Within its shell even ultimate nuclear heads stay safe as if hypnotized egg yolks No better space for us superhumans

Super risk-takers we drowned, burned, deleted borders Yet yearned To be seen as mere humans Not the way the word gets misused When they say human here they mean super- or sub-human It brings stromatolites to mind But that's a different testimony The first time we happened upon this land some eighty-six days ago we escaped becoming ice Unreal hyperreal Hull, Balzac, Edmonton, or some such Officials italicized us Offered a citizenship deal Cleansing tasks in homes infested by deadly duplicating virus

Save the elderly in this country

Unsilently we cried as they were crying unsilently The gatekeepers of placetime heard us as ambient biophonies or noise Our faces wore white Our bodies wore white Humming a forgotten melody If the germ spared us we hoped in overheated hospices (with sticky odours) we would finally be classified correctly In a mutilated world such a redress would have healed the healers The darkest prison is the one of discredited words Hope, Human, and some such So real we were And are Our repairing fingers almost touch a dream Ice sheets and ice fields nothing survives You will see only the dream survives

The day is running on low battery
Clouds of cicadas? Or
     lithium carts clearing little Rushmores
of snow? Thirteen shivering blackbirds
     play with a mirage
By the wide-eyed library
     a translated warning
—El río está peligroso
Swift-flowing a teacher projects
on a wall *Kisiskatchewanisipi* in Cree
     Gusts of recovered time
A funicular crawls up
     to the hotel with a wrong name
Sharp smells of pee & hashish
     muffle an underground stn
Soon tears might freeze
     but not arrested
Someone is listening to a Sahir Ludhianvi
     song and slips into warm flares
When night comes
     they will compete with flares that rise
     out of the oil refinery towers
by the river and the circle will complete it-
     self in a dream speckled with tar

PHOTOGRAPH OF MY FATHER
IN CIVILIAN CLOTHES

I.

So many dialogues I've had with the clothes
      and the styles of scarves
the young captain chose, but never tried
      to understand the one who did the choosing

Even then his face looked as if it could
      no longer recall the suffering
its younger versions endured
      As if it could only retain
memories that vibrate warm
      sensations into the ears of others

II.

Morning has arrived in my room
      In the photograph it is morning as well, my
      father and I have an entire day ahead of us

III.

The sun already strong No wind His civilian clothes flutter in the wake
of a train that just passed by
      I bend low
      I bend low until my ear lobe touches the metal
      of the track

IV.

In his shirt pocket a folded hand-
kerchief   and   a rarely used Montblanc

I ask why he chose not to translate
     what his body remembered?

Two thousand books live in his silences

Now two thousand books will never be written

Only once he said to me You are
          this photograph's dream
          you are its wish he said it
          softly that night long ago

ESHUVA
— for J.R. —

A bird left a mark
on my window   I wasn't inside
when it made pain-
ful contact with the glass
What do I know
about its pain   Was I trimming
the hedge then?
The chalky   mark appears
from certain angles like
Ichthyosaur
fossils I saw in a research lab
once   Today
when it vanished
in the morning fog
I felt
a need to see it again   gesture
to a neighbour
letting complete
silence convey
what language does not allow
Now the air is clear
again   again the bird
and it wants   something
from me
I try to sing an Eshuva but that's all
I do

O N C E

Once when I was a child I saw women who hugged
trees They hugged them as loggers
were only a pico-metre away
And the trees hugged the women back
an event not many noticed The air filled up with
sound treesound & tr ee sou nd
and   the whole earth   a thrum
The women are most likely dead and gone
by now But the trees remain

WHAT WILL YOU DO EARTH?

What will you do Earth when we are gone?
When we are gone will you miss us?

Systematically your geobiochem cycles
    will reorder & clean
what is left behind? "Our"
    objects will last   what we call a long
time Some will bring on other species
    unprecedented hardship
Eventually you'll make yourself
    that "delightful pristine wilderness"
    before we came along?
But who will show you the pictures
    of Earthrise as seen by your moon?
Who will make maps? And figure the whole
    project as plainwrong? Who will compose
    symphonies?
Who will sleep with rivers
    in dreams? Who will
allow forests to change one's heart?
    Who will worship your mountains?

Perhaps these are flawed questions
                        crumbling
mansions untouched
    by moss or remorse

When we are gone will you remember such remarkable
    creatures existed?
When we are gone will you miss us?

Each time a zooplankton swallows
    micro-plastic, a new couplet is born

Without interruption the sea
    composes cantos

of the Anthropocene   Scanned
    surfaces register other

styles of mutation   a sub-
    merged sonic   Finally poetry makes some

things happen   Rings
    colloids   stratigraphic offices   its new

forms   syntaxes   vocabularies
    Is the Earth dreaming   to take over?

In that old parable
    a grieving mermaid's tears turn

into tiny pendants of sea
    glass   and suspend

time The more
    plastic the zooplankton

swallow, the less
    they bloom   Does it

matter Make it old or new
  Make it living or unliving

The plankton are simply signalling
  to us the awakening

beats of the geobiochemical
  They'll only magnify   ahead

What we call beauty and sadness
  will outlast the language of the eon

and some acid or wave will dissolve
  the names we gave to things

In some strange countries not even clouds are allowed to remain as clouds. To make rain officials fire silver iodide bullets at clouds. Sixty billion cubic meters of water. In our country we fix droughts by knitting more and more clouds. Yet we fail to fathom them. Grandmother used to say they are calcium shawls wrapped around a dream. And we—who cannot live without likenesses—are often unable to tell if we are looking at them or at ourselves in a mirror.

DEW AND OTHER SOUNDS

Far away in Australia   camels and sapiens
compete   to collect dew   I hear
gutturals on ochre
tracks and dry pools
before the cull   usual
words   saviour and hero   but think
more and more about camels
                        and dew

Until all thinking washed
away and I was   as small
as a seed of urad

Perhaps some child in some Australian
city calls those shining drops moon-beads

I don't know I don't know how to end
the poem   neither does it
demand an ending

or shanti

Our youngest says
When we are gone
Other species will see us
In clouds

BEGINNING

Comes a time old phrases acquire new meanings
One looks at a loyal friend
an enlightened sibling
a beloved companion secretly
saying to oneself wouldn't it be nice
if I go first
If they go first I will go twice. First
with them then with myself. That is
a lot of goings

Comes a time when grief begins
although no one has gone yet

Short evening   It staggered   Spoke
in whispers   I almost broke bread
with a friend who left

before me   I am
cleaning the table   gazing at crumbs
of deep time

when the sea was Tethys and India parted
ways with Antarctica & Africa
                              and began

floating up North
like a raft   So far no sign
of the Himalayas

   In my small
room a
   bonsai

Only a few days ago
it gave up My arteries
and its capillaries nearly gave up

Today the bonsai appears
marked
by untranslatable happiness   Does it

mean
I too will soon feel
repaired?

News that stays news   comes
when I start dozing
off

Du Fu wrote
in the eighth century
The yin and yang of our existence

produced this storm and rain
I read again and admire
again   the bonsai

IKTSUARPOK

I'm cooking slow biryani and soon I'll be
headed to your place. I'd like to take
care of the nervous system of at least one
person. It's winter again we must talk about

winters. If views clash we'll practice
speaking untranslatable words

together, an Inuit noun, for instance, that sums up
the feeling that compels one to go outside and inside,
and outside and then inside again, to check if some-
one is walking over the hill or around the corner

We must keep revealing wounds as optional
—why we came here from there. How
hate grew like grass in every house

We'll skip clichés about hope to warm our interiors
Speculate about the future
of darkness and poetry Like three years ago we'll
skip dessert sip mint
                    tea   and listen

around the corner to the voices   voices
of neurons mending
                    voices
                    not yet called by that name

The persimmon
over his head
in the Muttart's
indoor garden

brought back the season
when he was almost

content
The rest of the day was
pure drag

Impossible to walk any-
where without socks

Yet he didn't
complain much
Earth

please ripen
your fruit
with sun and water as unhurriedly
as possible
Let him

savour reliving
the almostness

before he shares
with friends, non-friends, the full
Persimmon

Why do I keep returning to the silk cocoon
I held in my loose fist once   a child

I was then and the worm inside
the cocoon is still stirring

Why do I go on with the belief
hope's a leaf just about to turn

In Anthropocene what exactly is one

hoping for? How to *make hope possible
rather than despair convincing?*

I am listening to music made by a dead person
I am searching for a new language
A newspaper op-ed says
 —Hope tigers don't move into Mumbai
The music made by the dead person says
 —Let us not misuse hope
Tigers come because our living
 and the dead cremate forests

And why do I always assume hope is
non-violent time   it will recalibrate
my eyes, liberate me from history's silk & onions

Hope is delicate   it stumbles into a void
when one most needs it   I hope to finish
this page   One last time I hope to read it
when it is done

neither loudly nor quietly

Which is not the same as saying

every abandoned poem is
the densest shape
of hope   Polyp lips
                of unpublished rock
                    where the reef begins

p. ix: This book's epigraph comes from Li Po's, "Zazen on Ching-t'ing Mountain," translated by Sam Hamill. *Crossing the Yellow River: Three Hundred Poems from the Chinese* (BOA, 2000).

p. 5: The epigraph of "Coral Scientists" is from W.S. Merwin's *The Second Four Books of Poems* (Copper Canyon, 1992).

p. 7: For more on sapien emotions and the Great Oxygenation Event, see Dipesh Chakrabarty's *The Climate of History in a Planetary Age* (Chicago, 2021).

p. 13: Crawford Lake, Ontario. See *The Guardian* (11 July, 2023): "Canadian lake chosen to represent start of Anthropocene."

The quote at the beginning of the poem is from Tomas Tranströmer's *Half-Finished Heaven: Selected Poems* translated by Robert Bly (Graywolf, 2017).

p. 15: On March 5, 2024, I received a message from Dr. Helmut Weissert, earth scientist: "No official Anthropocene — It looks as if the Quaternary Working Group has rejected the proposal of the Anthropocene Group. No big surprise for me. Stratigraphers are the guardians of geologic time and many of them are, therefore, very conservative. Now the Anthropocene will exist as an informal term. But we can still call it an epoch."

p. 31: "… as if time were not a river but an earthquake happening nearby." From Roberto Bolaño's *Distant Star* translated from the Spanish by Chris Andrews (New Directions, 2004).

See Stephen Jay Gould's *Time's Arrow, Time's Cycle: Myth and Metaphor in the Discovery of Geological Time* (Harvard, 1988).

For more on ancient humans and "Odin Stone" like formations, see Hugh Raffles' *The Book of Unconformities* (Verse Chorus, 2020). A remarkable book.

p. 76: "Pavan guru Pani pita Mata dharat mahat" is from the Guru Granth Sa'ab. *Air/Wind/Breath our teacher   Water our father Earth our great mother*

p. 78: The quote is from: Andrew Y. Glikson and Colin Groves, *Climate, Fire, and Human Evolution: The Deep Time Dimensions of the Anthropocene* (Springer, 2016). "Having lost a sense of reverence toward Earth, there is no evidence humans are about to rise above the realm of perceptions, dreams, myths, legends and denial…"

pp. 81–95: This poem took its initial inspiration from the Abbas Kiarostami film *24 Frames*. "I've often noticed that we are not able to look at what we have in front of us unless it's inside a frame."

p. 83: Simon Schama's *Rembrandt's Eyes* (Penguin, 2015).

p. 88: Fracking in Rosebud. See Andrew Nikiforuk's *How Alberta Will Fight Fracking Folk Hero Jessica Ernst* (The Tyee, 16 Jan 2013).

p. 92: See Edward O. Wilson's *Half-Earth: Our Planet's Fight for Life* (Liveright, 2017).

p. 98: See Giorgio Agamben's *What Is an Apparatus?*, trans, David Kishik and Stefan Pedatella (Stanford, 2009). "To be contemporary means… to return to a present where we have never been."

p. 99: The demilitarized zone between North and South Korea. See Eric Wagner's *The DMZ's Thriving Resident: The Crane* (Smithsonian Magazine, April 2011).

p. 109: Chipko Movement in India in the 1970s. Chipko "to hug."

p. 118: The quote comes from *Du Fu: A Life in Poetry* translated by David Young (Knopf, 2008).

p. 119: The quote is from Ella Frances Sanders' *Lost in Translation: An Illustrated Compendium of Untranslatable Words from Around the World* (Ten Speed, 2014). Iktsuarpok sums up the "feeling that compels you to go outside and inside, and outside and then inside again, to check if someone is walking over the hill or around the corner."

p. 122: See Raymond Williams' *Keywords: A Vocabulary of Culture and Society* (Oxford, 1985). "To be truly radical is to make hope possible rather than despair convincing."

ACKNOWLEDGEMENTS

First versions of some poems appeared elsewhere:

"Tranströmer" and "Not Absence of Body" in *World Literature Today*, Jan 2024.

"Pause Me" in *Alberta Views*, Dec 2023.

"Coral Scientists," "Dream," and "Nubes, Clouds" in the inaugural issue of *Camel*, Dec 2023.

For known and unknown reasons I would like to thank Laurie Graham, Julie Robinson, Natania Rosenfeld, Helmut Weissert, Anton Kirchhofer, Kim Nekarda, Dionne Brand, Iman Mersal, Donna Kane, Sue Sinclair, Raúl Zurita, Forrest Gander, Mark Smith, Caleb at *Stop.gap*, David Martin, and Meredith Thompson. Special thanks to Matt Bowes for "commissioning a short piece" on Crawford Lake.

I am grateful to the Canada Council for the Arts.

In 2017, to honour NeWest Press' 40th anniversary, we inaugurated a new poetry series to go alongside our Nunatak First Fiction, Prairie Play, and Writer as Critic series: Crow Said Poetry. Crow Said is named in honour of Robert Kroetsch's foundational 1977 novel *What The Crow Said*. The series aims to shed light on places and people outside of the literary mainstream. It is our intention that the poets featured in this series will continue Robert Kroetsch's literary tradition of innovation, interrogation, and generosity of spirit.

CROW SAID POETRY TITLES AVAILABLE FROM NEWEST

Tar Swan — David Martin

That Light Feeling Under Your Feet — Kayla Geitzler

Paper Caskets — Emilia Danielewska

let us not think of them as barbarians — Peter Midgley

Lullabies in the Real World — Meredith Quartermain

The Response of Weeds: A Misplacement of Black Poetry on the Prairies — Bertrand Bickersteth

Coconut — Nisha Patel

rump + flank — Carol Harvey Steski

How to Hold a Pebble — Jaspreet Singh

Kink Bands — David Martin

Attic Rain — Samantha Jones

Dreams of the Epoch & the Rock — Jaspreet Singh

JASPREET SINGH is the author of several books including the 2021 memoir *My Mother, My Translator.*